LILLENAS®
DRAMA

Christmas Program Builder

No. 65

Compiled by Heidi Petak

lillenas®
PUBLISHING COMPANY
Kansas City, MO 64141

Questions? Please write or call:
Lillenas Publishing Company
Drama Resources
P. O. Box 419527
Kansas City, MO 64141
Phone: 816-931-1900 • Fax: 816-412-8390
E-mail: drama@lillenas.com
Web Site: www.lillenasdrama.com

Cover Design: Doug Bennett
Executive Editor: Heidi Petak
Supervising Editor: Kimberly Meiste
Manuscript Formatting: Karen Phillips

Contents

Preschool Recitations

Honoring the Christ Child

Bless us, Lord, at Christmas
And all the whole year through.
Help us honor the Christ Child
In all we say and do.

Dorothy Heibel

Ready!

My hands are ready to open my
gifts,
My mouth is ready to sing.
My heart is ready to welcome my
Lord
And worship Jesus my King.

Heidi Petak

Shhhhh!

We won't wake the baby because
He's asleep.
We'll tiptoe so quiet and not make
a peep.
But we're so excited baby Jesus is
here. *(Getting a little louder)*
We really can't stand it, *(Louder)*
We just have to cheer. *(Even louder)*
Yippeeeee! *(All cheer very loudly, then suddenly stop and put a finger over their lips)*
Shhhhh! *(Whispering)* The baby is
sleeping!

Heidi Petak

One-Two-Three Wise Men

(CHILDREN *hold up one finger, then two fingers, then three fingers whenever they say "one, two, three wise men.")*

One, two, three wise men filling
their packs, (CHILDREN *pretend to fill packs)*
Putting it all on three camel's backs.
(Hold up three fingers for camels)

One, two, three wise men travelling
far, (CHILDREN *walk in place)*
Following after a big, shining star.
(Hold up one hand, opening and closing like a blinking star)

One, two, three wise men kneeling
with joy, (CHILDREN *kneel)*
Bringing their gifts to the sweet
baby boy. *(Rock arms as if holding baby)*

One, two, three wise men know that
it's true. *(Children point to heads)*
That Jesus was born for me and for
you! *(Point to themselves, then someone else)*

Beth Swale

Recitations for Ages 5 to 10

Lamb of Light

Angels sang praises of
The perfect Lamb's birth.
The shepherds bowed low
Knowing His worth.

The little boy Jesus,
Born in the night,
Changed all the world
With the birth of His light.

Joy Shearer

A Christmas Gift

Ring the bells of Christmas,
Sing songs of *hope* and *love.*
The King of kings
And Lord of lords,
Our gift
From God above!

Dorothy Heibel

Room for Jesus

"No room here!" the innkeeper said,
Sending Mary and Joseph away.
No room could be found
To lay their heads
On that very first Christmas day.

But I will shout with all my might
And give my loudest cheer,
That Jesus has a place to stay
Because *(pointing to their hearts and shouting),*
There's room in here!

Heidi Petak

Christmas Star

(Readers may hold up signs with letters on them or the letters may be projected onto a screen.)

C – Can you imagine the brightest star ever?
H – Have you heard of the star that shone in the sky when Jesus was born?
R – Real people looked up and watched that star every night.
I – I wish I could have been one of those people!
S – So much light must have come from it night after night as it waited for Jesus' birth.
T – The people might have had to shut their windows to keep out the light.
M – Maybe some people thought the light was beautiful.
A – And maybe some people complained it was too bright for nighttime.
S – Some people may have wondered if it meant something special.
S – Some people may have wondered if it meant something bad.
T – That star just kept on going and going long enough for the wise men to find Jesus.
A – And then it stopped. And something wonderful happened.
R – Right under that star, the One who would save everyone . . . was born.

Beth Swale

Recitations for Ages 11 to 17

Holy, Holy, Holy

by Beth Swale

Close your eyes and keep them closed.
You've heard the Christmas story.
You know that Jesus came to earth as a baby.
You know He grew into a man who died for our sins.

But where was He before He came to earth as two cells in Mary's womb?
Do you think our minds can even imagine what He left behind?

Imagine the color gold, shining, gleaming, reflecting light.
Imagine the sound of huge wings beating up and down, up and down.
Imagine seeing creatures like nothing on earth with faces of lions and eagles and men.
Imagine hearing them calling out, "Holy, holy, holy is the Lord God Almighty, Who was, and is, and is to come!"

Imagine in all that golden light that you see a throne the color of emerald.
Seated on the throne is Someone so bright you can't see the details of His face.
A rainbow with colors our minds can't even fathom surrounds Him.
Seated on His throne, He is surrounded by twenty-four other thrones.
On those thrones are elders dressed in white and wearing golden crowns.
They fall down and worship the One on the emerald throne.
They take off their crowns and place them before Him.

Then they cry out, "You are worthy, our Lord and God, to receive
Glory and honor and power, for You created all things,
And by Your will they were created and have their being!"

Then the One on the throne, surrounded by light and glory and majesty,
Rises up and lets go of that honor and glory and power.
He is gone.

When we see Him next, He is a helpless baby, just born.
He is wrapped in strips of cloth and sleeping in a barn.
He will live and bleed and die so that we can join Him in glory.

"Holy, holy, holy is the Lord God Almighty, Who was, and is, and is to come!"

Gifts for the Holy Child

by Dorothy Heibel

The Christ Child lay on a bed of hay,
Bathed in heavenly light.
Mary and Joseph kept watch over Him
On that first Christmas night.

"Glory to God!" the angels gave
Their hymn of glorious praise,
Greeting the Child whom God had sent
To bring peace to our days.

The shepherds had no precious gems
Or heavenly songs to sing,
But they gave their loyalty and their love
To the baby Jesus King.

Then God gave light from a wondrous star
To lead the kings of old.
They worshiped the babe and gave Him gifts
Of myrrh, frankincense, and gold.

Like all of these, we too have gifts
For the babe Who came from above,
And when we give our loyalty
He gives us life and love!

White

by Heidi Petak

The snow falls gently to the ground,
Covering broken buildings, broken branches, broken bikes,
Blanketing the world in perfection,
In beauty,
In white.
A picture of God's forgiveness and grace
Come to earth as a gentle babe
To give His life,
And so His mercy falls on my soul,
Blanketing my brokenness,
Covering my sin with perfection,
With beauty,
With white.

Adult Readings

The Fullness of Time

by Kevin Stoltz

Now when the fullness of time had come, God sent forth His son, born of a virgin, born under the law. Close your eyes and listen to what you cannot see: the wind on a dark hillside and the smell of spring grass; the breath of the night air mingled with the smoke of a small fire; and the unmistakable sense of terror as frightened shepherds listen to the angels singing, "Peace on the earth, good will towards men." Listen. Do you hear beyond the shepherds, beyond the Bethlehem town, beyond the tiny kingdom of Judah, beyond the Middle East, beyond the past, beyond the future? Do you hear the pulse of the world, a pulse that beats endlessly, expectantly, hoping for something more?

The pulse of this world has a steady rhythmic beat; it is fear and uncertainty. Has the fullness of time come and gone? What of our time, and our place in the here and now? When we breathe in the night air, is there a hint of an angel's song? Would we be terrified of the heavenly host? If we saw the star in the east, would we follow? Would we care? *(Pause)*

The fullness of time has come, and it is now. Breathe in the night air, for the angel's chorus still lingers there. And it's OK to be terrified when the hosts of heaven sing, as long as you obey and follow the star in the east. Follow it to the end, and you will find the Babe, the Savior, the King, the One who is the Christ. The fullness of time has come, and it is Jesus, the Christ.

Christmas Morning

by Chris Baxter

Just before going off to bed on a wintery Christmas Eve, I took one last look at the glistening lights on the decorated tree. I loved how each little light sparkled in the darkness. My eyes, too, twinkled with delight as I studied the beautifully wrapped presents lying underneath the evergreen tree. Soon, each and every gift would be opened with glee. But for now . . . I must subdue the thrill of what lies ahead of me, turn, go to my bed, and face the long peaceful night.

Dressed in my Christmas pajamas, I reluctantly got under my covers and rested my head on my pillow; and then I dreamily thought of each gift that had my name written on the tag . . . the size, the shape, the mystery inside. How comforting to be loved by the giver of these gifts . . . how safe I felt *because of this love* . . . how securely I rested *in this love* . . . and then . . . I slept . . .

My eyes caught a hint of light coming from behind the shades of my bedroom window. Sitting up straight, I realized—*Christmas morning!* Happiness lifted me from my bed and quickly pulled me to the top of the stairs. Here, I impatiently waited for permission to race down and dive into each unopened gift—to finally hold each one, and then to embrace them as my own.

In the blink of an eye, I positioned myself before the tree. I gathered all the special gifts that bore my name. *"Which one should I open first?"* I asked myself excitedly. Eagerly, my hands grasped a square box wrapped in deep violet paper, tied with a bright red bow. The wrapping was so pretty, it almost seemed wrong to tear the paper. Yet, to take delight in any gift, the paper must be torn and the ribbon must be cut. So I proceeded, tearing the beautiful paper and lifting the lid. And there, before me lay . . .

the crown of life.

The crown was made of pure gold containing all sorts of jewels—rubies, diamonds, and sapphires throughout. With reverence, I pulled the crown from the box and placed it upon my head. My heart beat strong and my soul was overcome with . . . love.

"Who crowns you with lovingkindness and tender mercies."
Psalm 103:4 NKJV

My eyes then fell on the second gift. This one was wrapped in shiny, royal blue paper that glistened at each tilt and turn. A huge white bow rested on the top of the package. Again, opening it was a decision in and of itself—how beautiful the gift was! My fingers gingerly began to tear the paper until it was opened. Inside this box lay . . .

the blanket of peace.

As I pulled the soft, powder blue blanket from the box, I drew in a deep breath; I became so tranquil I could hardly understand it. How warm and comfortable the blanket felt as I wrapped it around my back and shoulders. I never wanted to leave this place. I would *always* be able to rest with this kind of peace surrounding my heart.

"Peace I leave with you, My peace I give to you; not as the world gives do I give to you. Let not your heart be troubled, neither let it be afraid."
John 14:27 NKJV

A bit overwhelmed, I slowly placed the third present in my lap. The box itself almost seemed vibrantly alive! All different colors zigged and zagged on the paper while the bright yellow, curly ribbon bounced on the top. With a grin, I observed this energetic wrapping and wondered with excitement what could possibly be inside. As I opened the present, there sat a wooden . . .

music box of joy.

To my sheer delight, the music box was designed the exact same as the gift box—all different colors splashed about. And then, when I lifted its lid, music like I had never heard before began to play—a mixture of hippity-hop-pity, rat-a-tat-tat music, plus the bouncy, bouncy clap, clap, clap music—the kind of music that makes you want to get up and dance. And so I did. I had the crown of life on my head . . . I was waving the blanket of peace all around and about me . . . and I was tap-dancing to the heartbeat of joy.

"These things I have spoken to you, that My joy may remain in you, and that your joy may be full." John 15:11 NKJV

A wee bit winded, I sat down to open up the next present. This one was in a shimmering silver gift bag with white tissue flowing from the top. I reached in the bag and pulled out . . .

the crystal goblet of living water.

Thirsty from my dancing, I took a small, curious sip from this exquisitely beautiful, sparkling goblet. The water was clear and pure and cool. How divine the drink tasted to my lips, and how refreshing the water was to my throat. I took another sip, and another, and another. I intended to drink the whole cup; but amazingly, the goblet never emptied!—An unending supply of living water was rewarded to this thirsty dancer of joy.

"Whoever drinks of the water that I shall give him will never thirst. But the water that I shall give him will become in him a fountain of water springing up into eternal life." John 4:14 NKJV

With awe and wonder, I selected yet another present from underneath the Christmas tree. The yellow paper around this box was almost blinding, and the bow was equally as bright. My heart and mind searched for what this gift might be. Once again I tore the paper and opened the box. From underneath the tissue, I pulled out the powerful . . .

lamp of wisdom and discernment.

As I held this sturdy lantern in my hands, I knew instantly that on the darkest night, in the darkest hour, this light would shine as bright as the noonday sun, calming all my fears and showing me the right way in which to direct my steps. As a matter of fact, I decided to test its power immediately; I couldn't wait until nightfall. So I took the lamp of wisdom and discernment in my hand, with my blanket of peace wrapped around my shoulders, wearing the crown of life upon my head, and marched to the sound of the now deep rhythmic drums coming from the music box of joy. I marched straight into the darkest closet in my house. And sure enough, the light overcame the darkness, and I rejoiced with singing.

"I am the light of the world. He who follows Me shall not walk in darkness, but have the light of life." John 8:12 NKJV

I could go on and on about my incredible Christmas morning. I was given roses that never wilted or lost their scent, a loaf of bread that always stayed warm and satisfied my deepest gnawing hunger, a golden key that could unlock any prison cell or any trap door in order to set any victim free! This key even fit into the gates of heaven . . . what more could I ask for?

"Oh, the depth of the riches both of the wisdom and knowledge of God! How unsearchable are His judgments and His ways past finding out!" Romans 11:33 NKJV

The last gift I opened was wrapped in ivory paper, decorated with a velvety-crimson bow. More than any other gift, I struggled with damaging this beautiful wrapping. Should I tear this paper in two and slice this magnificent bow? I could choose to leave the gift unopened and admire the beauty from the outside. But I knew in my heart, something more beautiful lay on the inside of this box. As I began to tear the paper, for some reason, tears began to well up in my eyes. Why this sudden sadness in the midst of such joy? What price was paid for this gift—and *all* the others? I humbly opened the box and beheld the simple, yet profound . . .

towel of immeasurable grace.

The hand towel was crimson red, just like the bow I cut. I picked it up and held it against my cheek. The plush thickness wiped away my salty tears. Then I looked a little closer. There, on the towel, was ***my name*** monogrammed in white! To be known intimately by someone who loves so extravagantly is almost too much for a human heart to take. Freedom wrapped in forgiveness—the indescribable gift!

"Come now, and let us reason together," says the LORD, "Though your sins are like scarlet, They shall be white as snow; Though they are red like crimson, They shall be as wool." Isaiah 1:18 NKJV

I sat speechless by the Christmas tree for a long time. Overwhelmed by the abundance of gifts around me I asked, *"**How** does someone love like this? **Why** have I been given this love? And **when** did this great love for me even begin?"* As I sat pondering these questions, I gazed deep into the evergreen tree; and there, nestled within the pine needles, I began to see the prominence of . . . the old rugged cross. Quietly, the answers to my questions whispered into my heart:

*"**How** do I love you? Let me show you the Way*

***Why**? Because I AM love . . . love that never fails . . . to give.*

***When**? I have loved you, my sweet child, from before the beginning of time. I loved you when I was lying in that manger, and I loved you when I was hanging on that cross.*

And I will love you forever more and more and more . . ."

Enjoy My gifts, each one.

Merry Christmas,

Emmanuel.

Sketches

These Hands

by Kathy L. Metzger

Running Time: 8 to 10 minutes

Themes: Christmas, Advent, Mary's Song, Salvation, Mother's Day

Scripture References: Luke 1:26-56

Suggested Uses: Sermon starter, Retreats, Classroom

Synopsis: Mary, the mother of Jesus, and a modern mother talk to their newborn infants; a parallel is drawn to the blessing of motherhood and the emphasis of Christ's ultimate purpose.

Cast:

MARY—A young mother, late teens to 20s
MOTHER—A modern-day woman in her late 20s to early 30s

Props:

Manger bed
Straw
Rocking chair
Two infants (or realistic dolls)

Costumes: Biblical-era outfit; modern-day woman's nightgown and slippers

Setting: Inside a home; Bethlehem, in a stable by a manger bed

Production Note: The scene will greatly be enhanced if real infants can be used; two realistic looking dolls will also work. Also, the use of lighting will greatly enhance the scene and help establish each space separately and as a whole, but no lighting is also a viable option. Lighting cues (LFX) have been included in the scene instructions to illustrate where lighting can be used to the fullest.

(An empty manger bed filled with straw sits CS. Off to the side, opposite the manger bed, sits a rocking chair. During the initial voice-over, two women enter. Both women are carrying a baby in their arms. One woman is MARY, *the mother of Jesus, dressed in biblical attire. The other woman, a first-time* MOTHER *is dressed in a nightgown and slippers.* MARY *kneels at the manger bed.* MOTHER *sits in the rocking chair.)*

VOICE-OVER *(can be pre-recorded narration, projected as a visual text on a worship screen or simply read aloud):* "My soul glorifies the Lord and my spirit rejoices in God my Savior, for he has been mindful of the humble state of his servant. From now on all generations will call me blessed, for the

Mighty One has done great things for me—holy is his name. His mercy extends to those who fear him, from generation to generation." (Luke 1:46-50) What manner of love is this?

LFX: *Soft light up on* MOTHER.

MOTHER *(softly singing):* "Silent night, Holy night, all is calm, all is bright . . ."

(Singing turns to a gentle humming as MOTHER *slowly rocks the infant in her arms. She speaks softly to sleeping infant.)*

All is calm tonight, isn't it, little one?

*(*MOTHER *leans back into the rocking chair and closes her eyes momentarily. She opens her eyes and looks out at an offstage window. Still speaking softly . . .)*

Oh, it's starting to snow. *(Speaking half to herself and half to sleeping infant)* It's so beautiful, looks like little specks of diamonds dancing to the earth. *(Full attention on the infant)* Looks like your first Christmas will be a white one. *Our* first Christmas together will be white.

*(*MOTHER *continues rocking the infant.)*

I still can't believe I'm your mommy. I don't know what I've done to deserve you. *(Playfully)* Can I tell you a little secret? *(Drawing the sleeping infant momentarily close to her mouth and whispering.)* I've never loved anyone more than I love you. *(Introspectively)* I've also never been more scared than I am right now. I've never been someone's mother before, and I'm scared I won't be everything you need me to be . . . that maybe I won't be able to keep you safe.

(Draws infant in close again and continues slowly rocking)

Right now you're in my arms and I can promise nothing's going to harm you, but I know it won't be like this forever.

LFX: *Lights up on* MARY. *Star appears above the manger bed and* MARY.

MOTHER / MARY *(overlapping dialogue, telescoping over the end of* MOTHER'S *previous line):* I'm going to have to lay you down and walk away.

MARY: But I promise I'll still be right here. *(Places sleeping infant into manger bed)* Oh, it's warm out here tonight. Maybe I've placed too many covers on You? *(Removes a cloth from infant, speaks softly)*

There you go. That's better, right? *(Looking intently at infant)* Look at You. My little boy! My Jesus. *(With disbelief)* I still can't believe I'm Your mother. *(Looks up toward heaven)* I don't know what I've done to deserve You. *(Looks to infant)* Can I tell You a little secret? *(Leaning close to infant)* I've never loved anyone more than I love You. *(Introspectively)* I've also never been more scared than I am right now. I guess I'm scared I won't be everything You need me to be . . . that maybe I won't be able to keep You safe. I've never been someone's mother before and You are a mystery, aren't You?

(MOTHER *starts slowly rocking and humming.)*

MARY *(to God):* O, Mighty One, You have done great things for me. My soul glorifies You, Lord, and my spirit rejoices . . .

(MOTHER'S *humming turns to singing.)*

MOTHER *(singing, telescoping over the end of* MARY'S *previous line):* "Son of God, love's pure light, Radiant beams from Thy holy face, with the dawn of redeeming grace. Jesus, Lord at Thy birth, Jesus, Lord at Thy birth."

(MOTHER *stops rocking.)*

MOTHER/MARY *(overlapping dialogue):* Sometimes all this seems so unreal.

MOTHER: And yet you're really here . . .

MARY: And everything's happening just as I was told it would . . .

MOTHER: You came right on schedule and you're perfect . . .

(MOTHER *and* MARY *both slowly remove the coverings on their infants and look at their child.)*

MOTHER/MARY *(overlapping dialogue):* Oh, I can't help but look at you . . .

MARY: Your two little feet with ten perfect toes . . .

(MOTHER *kisses the infant's hands.)*

MOTHER: Ten perfect little fingers . . .

MOTHER/MARY *(overlapping dialogue):* Two strong hands . . .

MOTHER: I wonder if you will be an architect, a sculptor, maybe a doctor? Whatever you do with your hands, I pray you will use them to love.

MARY: Oh, my son. My Lord, Emmanuel, whatever You do with these hands, I know You will use them to love.

MOTHER: Use them to love.

MOTHER/MARY *(together):* Use them to love.

LFX: *Lights out on* MOTHER *and* MARY; *a star visual transitions into a cross.*

(MOTHER *and* MARY *exit.)*

The Christmas Gift

by Gina Detwiler

Running Time: 15 to 20 minutes

Themes: God's gift of Jesus, Sacrificial gift of love

Synopsis: A woman who was given the greatest gift of all finds a way to give something back to the woman who sacrificed so much for her.

Cast:

MARGARET
JULIA—Margaret's sister
JANIE—Margaret's daughter

Production Notes: Musical clips are used to indicate the year, because there is a 20-year change from Scene 1 to Scene 2. [Use of clips less than 1 minute in length do not violate copyright laws.]

Because of time difference in scenes, in original performance, the same actress played young Julia and Janie (mother and daughter), while different actresses played Margaret and older Julia. Choose your actresses according to availability keeping in mind the importance of aging the characters.

Scene 1

(Opens in darkness)

SFX: "Don't Worry Baby" playing on radio

VOICE: Well, that was the Beach Boys with "Don't Worry Baby" from the movie *Good Morning Vietnam*, one of the biggest movies of this year. Well, that about does it for the top 100 countdown of the best of 1987. Hope you had a great year. Now, how about a little Christmas music to get you into the Christmas Spirit . . . "Jingle Bell Rock" by Johnny Mathis!

SFX: "Jingle Bell Rock"

(Lights up on MARGARET *as she is decorating the Christmas tree. She is humming along to the music, perhaps singing some lyrics.)*

SFX: Doorbell rings

MARGARET *(said in rhythm to music, may repeat several times):* Come in, come in, come in, come in . . .

*(*JULIA *enters with shopping bags.)*

JULIA: Margy . . . Margy!

*(*MARGARET *finally turns and sees who it is; turns down the radio.)*

MARGARET: Hey sis! What are you doing here?

JULIA: Just passing by. I tried to call but there was no answer.

MARGARET: Oh, I was just . . . had the radio on a little too loud, I guess. Sorry.

JULIA: You shouldn't just let people come in, you know. You never know what kind of crazy person may be out there.

MARGARET: Case in point. *(Laughs)* Seriously, what are you doing here? Don't you have to pick up the twins in five minutes?

JULIA: Yes, but they are having a class party today so the teacher said they would need to stay a little late.

MARGARET: I didn't know preschoolers were so tightly scheduled.

JULIA: Yes, well, I suddenly had fifteen minutes with *nothing* to do—you know how often that happens—so I thought I would stop by.

MARGARET: Well, that's a treat. Want some coffee?

JULIA: Love some. *(Sits while* MARGARET *goes off to get coffee)* You're tree looks beautiful, as always.

MARGARET *(offstage):* Thanks

JULIA: Your china angel collection has really grown.

MARGARET: Yeah, I picked up a few more this week at Kaufman's.

JULIA: I can't remember the last time I was able to put a china ornament on our tree. Now all our ornaments are made out of pinecones and popsicle sticks. Nothing breakable on the lower four feet. This year we couldn't find the Christmas angel for the top of the tree. It was a complete mystery. Then we were eating dinner last night and Tim looked up and noticed the angel was on top of the chandelier! Apparently the twins had wanted to see if she could really fly.

*(*MARGARET *returns with mugs and hands* JULIA *one. She also has a plate of cookies.)*

MARGARET: You really have your hands full with those boys. Look what I made last night.

JULIA: Snickerdoodles!

MARGARET: I had a craving for them.

JULIA *(tasting one):* I haven't had one of these in ages! I guess I'm going off my diet—for the third time today. Remember when we used to make them when we were kids?

MARGARET: Yeah. I remember you never let me roll them in the cinnamon.

JULIA: Because you rolled too hard and smooshed them. They looked like flat tires.

MARGARET: Yeah, but they flattened out when you baked them anyway. You were such a perfectionist about the snickerdoodles.

JULIA: I tried to show you the right way to roll the dough, but you refused to listen. "I do it by myself!" you would always say.

MARGARET: I should have listened, because you did turn out to be the best cook in the family. That's why Mom named you after Julia Child.

JULIA: And you were the smartest one in the family. That's why Mom named you after Margaret Thatcher. *(Eating)* I forgot how good these were. Do you have Mom's recipe? I need to make some with the boys.

MARGARET: Sure. I'll copy it for you. But are you sure you want the twins making cookies?

JULIA: These should be a little easier than the gingerbread men I made last year. I had them cooling on racks so that the boys could frost them, but they got to them first.

MARGARET: What happened?

JULIA: It was carnage! Gingerbread heads and severed limbs all over the kitchen! Not a pretty sight.

MARGARET: Oh no!

JULIA: They were very sorry after, but I decided, no more gingerbread men for a few years. But I still harbor this absurd notion that it would be fun to do Christmas cookies with the kids . . . they are almost three now. I think they can handle it.

MARGARET: Sure they can.

JULIA: I'm sorry, I shouldn't be talking about them so much . . .

MARGARET: Why not? They are your kids and they are beautiful.

JULIA: I know but it just reminds you of . . .

MARGARET: I'm OK, Julia. I'm getting there. I'm not saying it's easy to know that at the age of 26 I can never have a baby, but there are options. I sent away for some information about adoptions . . . we have to put in an application and there's a really long wait, but we've waited four years already . . .

JULIA: Margy, I have a confession to make. I didn't just happen to drop by. I came here today to . . . bring you something.

(Takes a gift out of the bag and gives it to MARGARET*)*

MARGARET: What's this? We exchange gifts on Christmas Eve, remember? Mom would kill us if we did it earlier.

JULIA: I know, but this is something I wanted you to have now. *(*MARGARET *opens gift, a small baby doll. She looks at* JULIA*, not understanding.)* I was trying to think of what I could give you this year for Christmas, and I know there is only one thing you really want. A baby. And since you got the news that you couldn't have one yourself . . . well, I went to see my doctor and asked him about being a surrogate for you. You know, to carry your baby for you. And he said I could do that, and I got all this information and I've checked it out very thoroughly . . . it will be yours and Greg's baby totally. That's what I want to do. I want to give you your baby. *(Pause)* Say something, Margy.

MARGARET: I don't know what to say. This is . . . kind of overwhelming. You would really do this for me? Be pregnant again for nine months?

JULIA: Well, I have to admit, I wasn't sure I really wanted to be pregnant again. But I want you to have a baby. I've prayed for it every night. So maybe . . . this is God's way of answering my prayers.

MARGARET: What about Steve?

JULIA: I talked to Steve. He thinks I'm crazy too, but he's being very supportive.

MARGARET: Julia . . . I can't let you do this.

JULIA: Yes, you can. You never were very good at letting me help you. But I want to do this. And anyway, it's my Christmas gift to you and you can't refuse it.

MARGARET: Oh Jules . . . I can't believe you would do this for me after I ruined your snickerdoodles.

JULIA: What are sisters for?

MARGARET: Thank you, Julia.

JULIA: You're welcome.

(They hug. Blackout)

Scene 2

(Present day, 2008; opens in dark)

SFX: "Mama Mia" on radio

VOICE: Well, there it was, "Mama Mia" by Abba, from one of the biggest movies of the year . . . Well, that's it for our year end retrospective, the Best of 2008. Now let's play some Christmas music to get into the Christmas Spirit . . . here's one of our favorites . . . "Jingle Bell Rock" by Pure NRG.

SFX: "Jingle Bell Rock"

(Lights up. Same room as in Scene 1, updated. JANIE *enters, looks around. She is twenty years old, carrying a book bag from school.)*

JANIE: Mom? Are you home? Hello?

JULIA *(offstage):* Who's here?

JANIE: It's me!

JULIA: Oh, hey Janie! It's me, Aunt Julia. I'm coming! *(*JULIA *enters wearing a robe and walking slowly. She sits in the chair.)* Your mom just went to pick up my prescription. She'll be back in a minute.

JANIE: Oh, did she take you to dialysis today?

JULIA: Yeah. Your Uncle Greg had meetings all day. Are you done with classes already?

JANIE: Yeah, thought I'd head to the mall, do some Christmas shopping before it gets all crazy.

JULIA: Good idea.

JANIE: Yeah . . . So how are you feeling?

JULIA: Oh, I have my good days. This doesn't happen to be one of them.

JANIE: Can I get you something? How about some tea? And I made snickerdoodles last night . . . oh, but I guess you can't have those, can you?

JULIA: No, doesn't go well with kidney disease. But tea . . . would be nice. Thanks. *(*JANIE *exits)* So your mom is still making you bake the snickerdoodles?

JANIE *(off):* Yeah. She says I have to keep up the tradition.

JULIA: Yes, I used to make Jared and Justin bake them, too. Until they finally rebelled at age 12.

JANIE *(off):* Jared and Justin . . . I haven't seen them in awhile. How are they doing?

JULIA: Oh, fine. Busy. Jared is headed to Nepal for Christmas. Some Mount Everest Adventure tour. Sounds like an awfully cold time to be in Nepal, but boys will be boys. But Justin said he was coming home for a couple of days. Probably needs his laundry done. *(Pause)* Your mom did a great job on the tree again. She always has the prettiest tree in the neighborhood.

JANIE *(off):* She's kind of a fanatic about her angels.

JULIA: Yes, I remember.

JANIE *(off):* She always made me and Dad wrap them in bubble wrap. It took forever.

JULIA: She loves her angels. I remember when she started collecting them. It was right after she and your dad got married.

JANIE *(returning with cup of tea):* Yeah, she told me it was because she wanted to have a baby. And the angels were like . . . the substitute or something until she got the real thing. She made me pose as an angel for the Christmas card every year until I was sixteen. It was so embarrassing.

JULIA: It was adorable!

JANIE: It was child abuse.

JULIA: You were her angel.

JANIE: But I was far from it. You know how I was.

JULIA: That's how teenagers are. It's a form of insanity. I always said I didn't want to have daughters because I knew what I put my mother through!

JANIE: It was just hard . . . living up to those angels.

JULIA: Well, you turned out just fine.

JANIE: Yeah, maybe. Is that OK? The tea, I mean.

JULIA: Fine. *(Winces)*

JANIE: Are you OK? I mean, does it hurt a lot?

JULIA: Sometimes. You get used to it.

JANIE: Yeah, I guess.

JULIA: So, how's college treating you? Almost done with finals?

JANIE: One more to go.

JULIA: Do you like it?

JANIE: Yeah. I guess.

(Pause)

JULIA: Hey, you have a birthday coming up, right? Twenty years old! I can't believe it.

JANIE: Yeah.

JULIA: Do you have plans?

JANIE: Not really. I mean, having a birthday on Christmas Eve kind of stinks because all my friends are already busy and we all have all the family stuff going on. So I'll probably celebrate after the holidays.

JULIA: Oh, well . . . good idea. Do something fun.

(Pause)

JANIE: Well, I'd better get going . . .

JULIA: OK. I'll tell your mom you were here.

JANIE: That's all right—I'll just text her. Are you sure you're OK?

JULIA: Yes, I'm good. Thanks for the tea.

JANIE: No problem. *(Starts to leave)* Aunt Julia?

JULIA: Yes honey?

JANIE: There's something I want to talk to you about. I was going to wait . . . but maybe . . . since Mom isn't here right now . . .

JULIA: What is it? Trouble at school? I know, you're dropping out. And you don't want to tell your mom. Is that it?

JANIE: Uh . . . no . . .

JULIA: Is it a boy? What am I saying, of course it's a boy! It's always a boy. What's his name? Doesn't your mom like him? Is he a Communist or something?

JANIE: It's not a boy.

JULIA: It's not a boy? Then what's wrong?

JANIE: Nothing, actually. Nothing's wrong. I just wanted to tell you that . . . Oh well, here. *(Pulls a small box from her book bag and hands it to* JULIA. JULIA *looks at the box.)*

JULIA: You're asking me to marry you? I don't think your mother will approve.

JANIE: Just open it.

*(*JULIA *sighs, opens the box. She stares at it, then lifts it out and holds it up. It's a small kidney bean.)*

JULIA: It's a . . . bean?

JANIE: A kidney bean. Get it? Well, it's supposed to represent a kidney. A real kidney. I thought this would be . . . I don't know . . . cute. It's stupid, I guess.

JULIA: Janie, I don't understand.

JANIE: I'm giving you a kidney.

(Pause)

JULIA: Why?

JANIE: Because you need one. And I've got two. And I happen to be a match.

JULIA: You got tested?

JANIE: Yeah.

JULIA: Why?

JANIE: Because! I just told you. I want to give you a kidney. It's a Christmas present. So you can't refuse.

JULIA: Honey, you are so young, you're in college. You can't take that kind of time off to donate a kidney . . .

JANIE: I've got a month off over Christmas.

JULIA: You want to blow your whole Christmas vacation in the hospital?

JANIE: Yeah.

JULIA: That's really sweet, honey . . .

JANIE: Aunt Julia, if it weren't for you, I wouldn't even be here. I mean . . . I wouldn't even be alive.

JULIA: What do you mean?

JANIE: I mean, I know what you did. Mom told me.

(Pause)

JULIA: She wasn't supposed to do that.

JANIE: She went to get tested, but she wasn't a match. And she was really sad about that. That's when she told me. At first, I couldn't believe it. You know, I'm twenty years old, an only child, I've pretty much gotten my way my whole entire life. I could never imagine making that kind of sacrifice for someone else. I've never had to. But what you did for Mom . . . it's kind of like what Jesus did for us, in coming down to earth. I was thinking about that, how He was the King and probably lived in a palace in heaven, and He gave up all that to come down here, to be cold and hungry and homeless and abused and killed . . . all for love. That kind of love . . . it blows my mind, honestly. I don't know if I have that. But I want to try.

JULIA: Janie . . .

JANIE: Please don't say no. Because this is the one and only time in my life I have ever done something for someone else, and I can't blow it now. You know what I mean? And I'm kind of scared too, so if you give me a chance to back out, I probably will, and then you'll end up going to dialysis three times a week for the rest of your life or until someone else steps forward with a kidney. And if someone else can do it, then so can I.

JULIA: I don't know what to say.

JANIE: Say "thanks." Or say "Gee, Janie, that is just about the best gift anyone has ever given me and I'll be grateful to you forever, and I may even buy you a car."

JULIA *(laughing):* Do you know why your mother named you Jane?

JANIE: Because she wanted to give me some boring name that I would hate?

JULIA: No. Because the name Jane means, "Gift from God." That is what you were. It seemed appropriate that you were born the day before Christmas. We didn't plan it that way, but I think God did.

I did give birth to you, and I loved you from the first like one of my own, even though I knew you weren't really mine. But I got to hold you in those first few minutes, and I looked into your eyes, and I knew there was a part of you that would always be mine. Just a little part.

JANIE: Well, see? Now you get a real part of me. One of my best parts, actually.

JULIA *(laughs):* Thank you, Janie. This is the best Christmas gift I have ever gotten. Except for one.

JANIE: Well, Merry Christmas, Aunt Julia.

JULIA: Merry Christmas.

(They hug as lights fade to black.)

Monologue

The Shepherd's Tale

by Gordon Williams

Running Time: 4 to 5 minutes

Scripture Reference: Luke 2

Synopsis: The nativity as seen through the eyes of one of the shepherds present during the birth of the Christ Child, an event which changed his life forever.

Cast:

SHEPHERD—A man in his 50s

SHEPHERD: Listen, brothers of Bethany! Lend me your ears! I hail from Bethlehem, and I have a story to tell! A story that began 30 years ago in that little town. Have you not heard?

I was but three and twenty years of age then, out in the field with my father and uncle tending our sheep. It was an ordinary night, stars blinking at us, a blazing fire to keep us warm. We were all wearing at least three layers of woolen garments, but I was still shivering and kept close to that fire whenever I didn't have to go out in the field to check on our flock.

We three were huddled together when suddenly a blinding light appeared above us. We shielded our eyes and squinted and looked, and there he was! *(Holds up his hand)* Yes! I speak the truth! We didn't know who he was, or what he was, but he was surrounded by a light, a powerful light like we'd never seen before. When I realized he was an angel, I was terrified!

But he assured us, "Do not be afraid! I bring you good news of great joy that will be for all the people. Today in the town of David a Savior has been born to you; He is Christ the Lord. This will be a sign to you; you will find a baby wrapped in swaddling cloths and lying in a manger."

And then a whole company of angels appeared behind him, declaring, "Glory to God in the highest, and on earth peace to men on whom His favor rests." Then the angels left and returned to heaven!

We all looked at each other. Did that really just happen? My uncle was the first to speak, "Let's go to Bethlehem and see this thing that has happened, which the Lord has told us about!"

My father was excited. "Yes! Let's go! Grab the woolen blankets, son; the Child might need them."

I grabbed the blankets and we ran into town. Augustus was emperor of Rome and he had ordered a census. That meant every man had to return to the place of his birth to be registered.

We thought perhaps the mother of the baby might be a traveler and decided to check the only inn at Bethlehem first. But when we told the innkeeper we were looking for a baby, the Christ Child, he shook his head. Then his wife beckoned us.

"Come with me," she whispered, leading us outside to the back. "A girl came here tonight about to deliver. You may find a baby there." She pointed to a grotto they used to keep livestock. I thought, "The Son of God—born in a cave?"

She looked embarrassed. "We had no room available. They all had been taken by the time the couple got here. This was the best we could do." She called out as we approached, "Hello? I'm sorry, but you have visitors!"

A young man came to the entrance. He was about the same age as I, judging from his appearance, and he was obviously perplexed.

"We have come to see the Christ Child," said my uncle. "We know He was born this night. Might He be here?"

The young man nodded. "Yes, He is here," and he turned and led us into the cave.

My heart leaped in my chest. And suddenly, there He was! Just as an angel told us, the Baby was wrapped in nothing but swaddling cloth, lying in a common feeding trough.

His mother was kneeling beside Him, singing. We threw ourselves to the ground beside her, lifting our hands and voices in praise to God.

The young man knelt next to me and whispered, "But how did you know? How did you know where to find us?"

Then we told him of the angels out in the field; that they were the ones who told us about the birth of the Christ Child, and how we could find Him.

Then we gave them the blankets. "It's the best we can do," explained my uncle. "We are only shepherds. We don't have much."

The mother seemed grateful for our small offering. "God will surely bless you," she said. "We will use the blankets tonight."

We bowed again, and went out. As we walked back to our flock, skipped, actually, we couldn't believe that we had been invited to the birth of the Christ Child.

None of us were ever the same after that night. And we have spent the last 30 years telling others what we saw in that grotto, as I am telling you know.

(Pause)

But I must tell you the rest of the story. Two years after that night, something terrible happened. King Herod ordered every male child in

Bethlehem under two years of age to be killed. I lost my own son that night. My wife never recovered from it; she died of grief.

I believe Herod was after the Christ Child. He wanted His life. And I don't know how, but the couple must have been warned of the danger and fled from Bethlehem when they had the chance. I just knew in my heart that the Christ Child was still alive.

Today, I believe that Christ is none other than Jesus the Nazarene, who I heard just a few weeks ago healed an official's son at Capernaum. It has to be Him. I hope one day I will see Him again, face-to-face. But no matter. I will continue to tell the story of that night I saw Him in that manger in the grotto as long as I live!

Christmas Service Idea

The First Christmas

by Rheta Perez

Running Time: 45 minutes to an hour

Scripture Reference: Luke 2; John 3:16

Synopsis: Bethlehem at the time of the census ordered by Caesar Augustus; time of Jesus' birth

Cast:

NARRATOR—Tells the Christmas story to the audience
MARY—Mother of Jesus
JOSEPH—Mary's husband
MATTHEW—Sara's son, age around 6 or 7
SARA—Adult female, Matthew's mother
CALEB—Sara's husband
SHEPHERD 1—Hears the heavenly host regarding Jesus' birth
SHEPHERD 2—With the first shepherd who hears the heavenly host

Production Note: There are a number of non-speaking parts. The number was deliberately left out depending on availability of actors. The scenery should be simple and requires only two sets. The choice of Christmas songs are suggestions and up to the discretion of the director.

Scene 1

(Before the lights go up, the choir is singing a Christmas carol, "Joy to the World." Congregation may join them. Lights up on NARRATOR *as the song ends.)*

NARRATOR *(reading from Luke 2):* In those days Caesar Augustus sent out a decree that a census should be taken of the entire Roman world. And everyone went to their own town to register. So Joseph also went from Nazareth to Bethlehem the town of David, because he belonged to the line of David. He went there to register with Mary, who was pledged to be married to him and was expecting a child.

(Stage lights come up on a crowded market place in Bethlehem; so many people around it is hard to move. MATTHEW, *a small boy about six or seven, is standing CS. He is very unhappy because he has lost his mother. The crowd ignores him for the most part, merely stepping out of his way. As he begins to cry,* MARY *and* JOSEPH *enter from SL.* MARY *is obviously very pregnant and* JOSEPH *walks her to the one*

spot without so many people. As MARY *starts to sit down, she sees* MATTHEW, *who is now crying loudly.)*

MATTHEW: Mommy! Mommy!

MARY *(walks over to* MATTHEW *with* JOSEPH*):* What's the matter, little one? Are you lost?

MATTHEW: No, but my mommy is!

MARY: We'll help you find your mommy. What is her name?

MATTHEW: Mommy.

*(*MARY *and* JOSEPH *look at each other and smile.)*

JOSEPH: What does your mommy look like? I'll go look for her.

MATTHEW: She's the most beautiful mommy in the world. And she got lost. And so did my blankie.

*(*JOSEPH *exits.)*

MARY: I'll bet she's looking for you. Do you want me to stay with you until she comes back?

MATTHEW *(sniffles and nods):* And I want my blankie.

MARY: Is it your favorite?

MATTHEW: Yes.

MARY: I'll bet it will turn up, too.

*(*MARY *and* MATTHEW *sit down on a bench. It is still very crowded, but* MATTHEW *stays close to* MARY. MATTHEW *accidently touches* MARY'S *swollen belly.)*

MATTHEW: Boy, you sure have a big belly!

MARY *(laughs lightly):* I'm going to have a baby. And I think He wants to see His mommy soon too.

MATTHEW: What's your name?

MARY: Mary. What's your name?

MATTHEW: Matthew. Do you think your dad will find my mommy?

MARY *(chuckling):* You mean my husband? Oh, yes, I'm very sure. We'll just wait right here.

*(*MARY *and* MATTHEW *sit together for a few moments.* MATTHEW *has stopped crying and holds on to* MARY'S *hand. Choir sings another carol, "O Little Town of Bethlehem." Congregation may join them.* SARA, *who is extremely agitated, followed by* JOSEPH *runs on stage to* MATTHEW, *carrying his blankie.* SARA *picks up* MATTHEW *and hugs him.)*

MATTHEW: My blankie! *(Takes it from* SARA.*)*

SARA *(kissing* MATTHEW'S *forehead):* I was so worried. Are you all right?

MATTHEW: I'm fine, Mommy. This nice lady sat with me. Isn't she beautiful? She's as pretty as you.

SARA *(to* MARY*):* Thank you so much for finding Matthew and helping him not to be afraid. I'm Sara. Are you from Bethlehem?

JOSEPH: No, we just arrived for the census. My name is Joseph and this is Mary. There are so many people here. My wife is about to have a baby. Do you know where we might get a room?

SARA: I don't know. There is an inn about two blocks from here. *(Points in the direction of SL)* You could try there.

JOSEPH: We just came from there. There aren't any rooms available. Everyone's come in for the census.

SARA *(concerned about* MARY'S *condition):* I wish we had room at our house, but we have so many relatives visiting that there isn't even room on the roof.

MARY: That is very kind of you to offer, and even if you had room, we couldn't impose. I'm sure we'll find something soon. God will provide.

SARA: I'm so sorry. You were so nice to Matthew. I wish I could help you.

MATTHEW *(tugging on* SARA'S *sleeve):* Mommy! What about the stable where Daddy keeps the animals?

SARA: Honey, a stable is a place for animals, not people. But it is better than sleeping on the streets, isn't it? I can give you some blankets. Would you mind sleeping in a stable? I mean, you're having a baby.

JOSEPH: If a stable is God's provision, we are grateful. Thank you. I can pay you for the room.

SARA: Oh no! Of course not. I feel bad just offering it to you, it's not much of a room.

MARY: This is an answer to our prayer. Praise God! And may God bless you for your kindness.

SARA: I need to go by my house first to get the blankets. Come with me and I'll take you there. You must be hungry and I can give you a little something to eat.

*(*SARA, MATTHEW, Mary *and* JOSEPH *exit SR. As the lights go down, the choir sings "Away in a Manger." Congregation may join them.)*

Scene 2

(Stage is divided into three sections: the area where the shepherds are on far SL, the manger scene with MARY *and* JOSEPH *on far SR, and CS which is busy Bethlehem. The manger scene is lit while the rest of the stage is black.* SARA, MATTHEW, *and* CALEB *are taking* MARY *and* JOSEPH *to the small stable, crossing from CS to far SR. Inside the stable, near the manger,* SARA *and* MATTHEW *spread out the blankets on*

the floor. CALEB *carries a lamp which is their only source of light and places it on a small make-shift table.)*

SARA: I told you it wasn't much, but at least you will be warm and dry.

JOSEPH: I don't know how to thank you.

CALEB: Please, Joseph, it was your kindness in taking care of our lost little boy. I wish we had room in our house, but . . .

MARY *(smiling):* We thank God for your generosity.

SARA: If you need anything, please ask.

CALEB: Peace be with you.

JOSEPH: And also with you.

MATTHEW: Mommy, Daddy, can I stay with them for awhile? Please?

SARA: No, darling. See, the mommy is very tired. She needs to rest. But you can bring them something to eat tomorrow.

MATTHEW: Please? *(Looks at* SARA *who gives him the look)* OK. *(To* MARY.*)* I'm going to bring you breakfast!

MARY: That would be wonderful. Thank you. I'll see you tomorrow.

*(*CALEB, SARA, *and* MATTHEW *leave, but not before* MARY *hugs* MATTHEW *and kisses him on the forehead. Lights go down as choir sings "Silent Night." Congregation may join them.)*

Scene 3

(Lights rise on the shepherds. An angel appears who pantomimes what the NARRATOR *is saying. As the* NARRATOR *explains the scene, the angel is joined by the heavenly host who sing "Glory to God in the Highest!" This can be a longer arrangement for a quartet or a simple melody sung with the phrase.)*

NARRATOR: And that night, there were shepherds in the fields, taking care of their sheep, when the angel of the Lord appeared to them and told them of the miraculous birth of the Messiah, the promised One. Then, with the angel, there appeared a heavenly host praising God and singing, "Glory to God in the highest!" The shepherds were so excited that they left their sheep and went to find the newborn King.

(Stage becomes dark and then a bright light goes on over the stable. Several shepherds run to the stable, but do not go inside.)

SHEPHERD 1: Hello in there!

JOSEPH *(stands and greetings them):* Yes?

SHEPHERD 1: You ain't gonna believe this, but my brothers and I were just out there with them sheep and all of a sudden there was music and light and angels! They were everywhere! They told us that the Savior, the Messiah was born in the city of David. The Messiah! Is He here?

*(*JOSEPH *steps aside so that* MARY, *who is holding an infant, can be seen.)*

MARY: This is Jesus.

SHEPHERD 2: The Messiah?

MARY: It is He.

(Shepherds fall to their knees and pay homage to the baby Jesus. Choir sings "While Shepherds Watched Their Flocks." Congregation may join. MATTHEW *then enters, carrying his blankie and a basket full of food.)*

MARY: Matthew! How good to see you! Come, see my baby. *(*MATTHEW *timidly steps forward and sits by* MARY *and the infant.)* Isn't He beautiful?

MATTHEW: He's so little. Was I ever this little?

MARY: I'm sure you were.

MATTHEW: He's pretty. *(He gently touches the infant's hand, then kisses him on the forehead. He gives* MARY *his blankie.)* This is my blankie. I want to give it to your baby so He won't get cold.

MARY *(taking the blanket, she wraps the infant in it):* Thank you so much, Matthew. See, the Baby smiled at you. He likes your blankie.

MATTHEW *(kisses the infant on the forehead again):* Happy birthday, baby! You are a special baby. I love You. And I will never forget You.

(Lights fade and the choir sings a carol, "O Holy Night." The congregation may join them.)

NARRATOR: The whole world changed that special night. The night the promise of our Lord God was fulfilled with the birth of His only Son, Jesus Christ. The Redeemer, the Son of God; the Messiah. Our Savior. Because God loves us so much He gave us His only Son, who died so that by believing in Him, we can all have eternal life. Amen.